Powerful Beginners Guide To

Dominate Binary Options

Jordon Sykes

Table Of Contents

Introduction 3

Chapter 1: Basics Of Binary Option Trading 9

Chapter 2: Getting Started 20

Chapter 3: Key Concepts for Beginners 30

Chapter 4: Binary Options Strategies 44

Chapter 5: Binary Options Strategies And Techniques For Beginners 57

Chapter 6: Beginner Binary Options Winning Strategy 70

Conclusion 77

Introduction

Binary options are also known as digital options. They are a simple and easy way to track price fluctuations in the global markets. However, the trader needs to understand the risks as well as rewards of these instruments as they can have a great impact on your finances. It's very important to understand that binary options are quite different from various traditional options. When you indulge in the trade, there are different aspects involved including investment process, risks, fees, and payouts. When you consider hedging or speculation, binary options form a great alternative; nevertheless, you need to understand the potential outcomes of these great options.

This is a relatively new financial trading system with two possible outcomes, that's why it's called Binary Options. There is no actual trading taking place, but a trader needs to guess whether the market value of a particular asset will go up or down in a given period of time. For a correct guessing, the trader earns a fixed payout while for a wrong guess he or she will lose the money invested by him or her.

What determines the success in this trade?

Learning is the key since one can gain or lose for his/her assessment of market movements of the assets. It requires lots of efforts to develop an insight to be successful in Binary Options trading. There are few important things that a new trader must know about:

- **Binary Options Broker**: A trader needs to find a broker who will provide him/her with the services to access the global financial market for the trading.

- **Demo Account:** Most brokers provide a demo or practice account which a trader can use for demo trading without investing their real money.
- **Trading Platform:** The broker provides its clients traders with a trading platform through which one can access the financial market and can start trading.
- **Financial Assets:** These are the listed tradable instruments on which one can invest money. They may include forex, stocks, commodities, etc.
- **In-the-money:** When a trader guesses the asset movement correctly, he or she earns a fixed payout, which is called in-the-money.
- **Out-of-money:** Many brokers provide a out-of-money protection to their traders. This ensures that even if a trader fails in his/her trade, he/she will not lose all the invested money. Under this arrangement, a pre-decided percentage of investment remains protected in case of a wrong assessment.
- **Technical Analysis & Tools:** Most brokers provide their traders with different types of technical tools, helping them to make profitable trades. These tools include trade alerts, market reviews, technical charts, historical data, news and updates and a host of other resources.

In Binary Options, executing trades is rather simple but making a correct decision often requires a lot of homework. This is the reason why it is more challenging for a beginner. There are a lot of things to learn and the above-mentioned pointers can merely provide someone with a basic idea about the exciting world of Binary Options trading.

Binary options are often classified as exotic options, yet the binaries are very easy to use. As they provide access to the foreign exchange, indexes, stocks as well as commodities they can also be termed as fixed return option or FRO. This is due to the reason that these options have got an expiry time which is known as the strike price. In case a trader wagers rightly in the direction of the market and the price at the expiry time is in sync with the strike price, the trader is paid a fixed amount of return irrespective of how much the financial instrument moved. On the contrary, a trader who wagers wrongly in the direction of the market, loses a fixed amount of his or her investment.

If any trader believes that the market is touching the higher side, he will opt for a "call." On the other hand, in the case of a fall in the market he will opt for a "put". In the former case, the price of the instrument must be above the strike price at expiry time, whereas in the case of the latter it should be below the strike price. All the aspects including risk, strike price, expiry as well as payout are disclosed at the outset of trading. The only things that may fluctuate in the market are the risk and payout.

Binary options are a great alternative for hedging or speculation and they come with some advantages and disadvantages. Some of the most common plus point of these options are no commission, known rewards and risk, innumerable strike prices and customized investment amounts, whereas the disadvantages, include limited regulatory oversight, lesser winning payout as well as non-ownership of any assets. Traders just have to be sure that they have got adequate knowledge of this form of investment so as to avoid losses

With the growing awareness around Binary Options trading, more and more newbie traders are getting attracted towards this financial trading arena. But traders who don't have any expertise in trading financial assets, Binary Options could be a complex financial instrument for them. However, significant profits are guaranteed at a minimal investment and at a fairly speedy manner, if someone learns the ins and outs of this new trading system. Thus, it's important for a beginner to gain some knowledge in order to stay profitable in their trading.

Binary options trading is often considered a very risky option for many these days. People who are new to the concept of trading often make the mistake of choosing digital trading to start their trading endeavor. Before long, they realize they have done a terrible mistake, but by then, it will be too late to go back. We are not trying to scare you off here, but caution and research can help you go a long way in this industry.

The return that you can get from this trading depends a lot on your choices. You might get a fixed return, a return in the form of an asset and at times, nothing at all. One drawback associated with binary options trading is that you have almost no chance of getting a refund. It is in your best interest that you talk to an expert or a friend with considerable experience in trading before you venture into this business.

As a beginner, one should invest lots of time in doing researches and understanding more about this. One can make use of a binary options forum to know more about it. There are various aspects that you need to be aware of. As you go along, you will learn new things and there is absolutely no substitute for experience in this trading form.

To start with binary trading, one needs to open a new account. You can seek the assistance of various online brokers to get yourself started. You will find a lot of websites that offer brokerage services for beginners. An online broker can also help you in choosing which asset to trade upon. Since there are lots of assets to choose from, an expert advice should be more than welcome.

But you cannot rely on your online broker to make all decisions for you. You need to base your decisions on extensive researches and knowledge that you have gathered from expert traders. One needs to keep themselves updated with all the changes happening in the industry. They should be aware of the market conditions at all times. By closely observing the trends of the market, one can learn a lot of new things that others might not tell you. Remember, everyone is here to make money and they would not risk it by sharing their secret with you. Binary options trading can be a lucrative career if you get your basics right and do not take many risks at the beginning.

Binary options trading is a new type of trading method which has won a lot of fans in a very short time. The concept is quite simple; you predict if the value of a particular asset will go up or down. If you make the prediction correctly, you stand to win a lot of money. On the other hand, if your predictions turn out to be a wrong one, you might lose a part of your investment. The world of trading is a highly volatile one. Trends and values can change numerous times in the course of a day. This makes it imperative for traders to be connected to the trading world at all times.

Anybody with a basic understanding of trading can try their luck at binary options trading. However, people with a deep understanding of the market tend to make lesser mistakes, and hence their returns will be higher than the beginners. Another important aspect of this trading is that there are many online broker platforms available that can help such people make wise decisions. This also comes with the advantage that you can trade from anywhere in the world at a time of your choosing. All you need is a computer and an internet connection.

If you are someone who is trying to start a career in binary options trading and is looking for resources to know more about it, you can use the internet for it. There are numerous blogs and forums available online which exclusively deal with this topic. Here, you will get to see an accurate picture of the business because nobody is trying to sell anything. They are expressing their opinions and sharing their experiences. One thing you will learn from it is that this form of trading is a very productive one if you make your moves diligently and carefully. Like any other business, there are numerous risk factors involved here too. But, there are certain things that you will learn only with experience. Therefore, you should not back off just because you had a couple of downfalls.

The best way to succeed in this trading is to learn as much as you can about it. You will find lots of information in this guide which will provide you with all the details you need to know about binary options trading.

There are various jargons pertaining to this business. For a beginner, it will not mean much at the beginning, but it is vital that they spend the time and effort to learn it. This is because all seasoned traders will be using such terminologies to address a situation. It would not be too bright of you to ask for translations every now and then. The sooner you become comfortable with the trading terminologies, the better!

The greatest advantage that this trading offers is the clarity in profits and losses. You will know right from the beginning how much you can earn and how much you might lose. This allows you to be better prepared for the best or worst.

Chapter 1: Basics Of Binary Option Trading

Binary options are very simple option contract with a fixed risk and fixed reward. These options are called binary options because there is a "one or the other choice" and a one or the other payout after the option expires. One or the other choices include up or down, or touch, and no/touch. In computer code binary means 1 or 0, or one or the other.

The way binary options works is from the traders perspective (yours); you choose whether or not a certain underlying asset (a stock, commodity, currency etc) is going to go up or down in a certain amount of time. You essentially bet money on this prediction. You are shown how much money up front you will earn if your prediction is correct. If your prediction is wrong, you lose your bet and the money is risked. If you predict correctly you get your money risked back PLUS a return. These returns usually are between 70-85%.

A brief example would be that you predict the price of gold to rise from it's current price of "$1612.75" one hour from now. The winning trade offers a return of 80%. You place a $100 trade on this idea.

One hour from now the option contract expires (closes) and the contract is graded as a "win" or a "loss", or "in the money" / "out of the money". Gold goes up to $1613, you predicted correctly. You get your $100 back and a return of 80% – or $80 for a total of $180. Even though gold only went up a tiny amount, you still earn the 80% return. The magnitude of price movement is not a factor in the amount of your return.

Key Ingredients Of A Binary Option Trade

All of the different binary options contracts have these three key ingredients that traders need to take note of. They are the expiry time, the strike price, and the payout offers.

- Expiry Time
- Strike Price
- Payout Offer

The expiry time is simply the length of time from the moment you 'buy' the option contract until it closes. This can be as fast as 60 seconds or as long as a month. The majority of traders are trading the short term binary options, anywhere from 60 seconds to 30 minutes.

The strike price is the price that you were able to enter the trade at, and this is the price that determines whether or not your trade is a winner or a loser. In the brief example above, the strike price is $1612.75. This is the price that gold needed to close at above in order to win this trade.

The payout offer is the return that binary options broker is offering to you. In the gold trade example above, the payout offer was 80% for a win and 0% for a loss. Some trades do have a return percentage for losses, typically up to 10% although this is broker and trade dependent. The payout offer is known up front before risking any money.

Types Of Binary Options Available

There are multiple types of binary options available to trade. The simplest and by far most common trade is the Up/Down trade. You can learn about the different types of binary options available to trade here.

Beginner Strategies

We have compiled a list of basic binary options strategies that will help you get started on making higher probability trades.

Tools You May Want To Use

I am going to beef up this section as new tools arrive on the market to help you make your trades. For now, you can review some of the binary trading signal services on this page.

Key Things To Know About Binary Trading

So now you understand the basics of trading binary options. Some key things you should remember before you dive in are:

- Your risk is limited to your trade amount
- The minimum trade is as little as $10
- You do pay for losing trades – you lose your trade amount (or the majority of it)
- There is plenty of risks involved. Never ever invest more with a broker than you can afford to lose. It's risky!
- You never take any ownership of the underlying asset – you only "bet" on the direction of its price movement
- To make money over the long term you have to win the majority of your trades
- Up / Down are only 1 type of binary option, there are many different kinds of trades available to make with binaries

Trading binary options are designed to be easy to do.

Your risk is limited to the amount you place on the trade. Your payoff is clearly stated before making the trade. If you win a binary options trade, you win a fixed amount of cash. Since there are only two possibilities, that's the origin of the name "binary options."

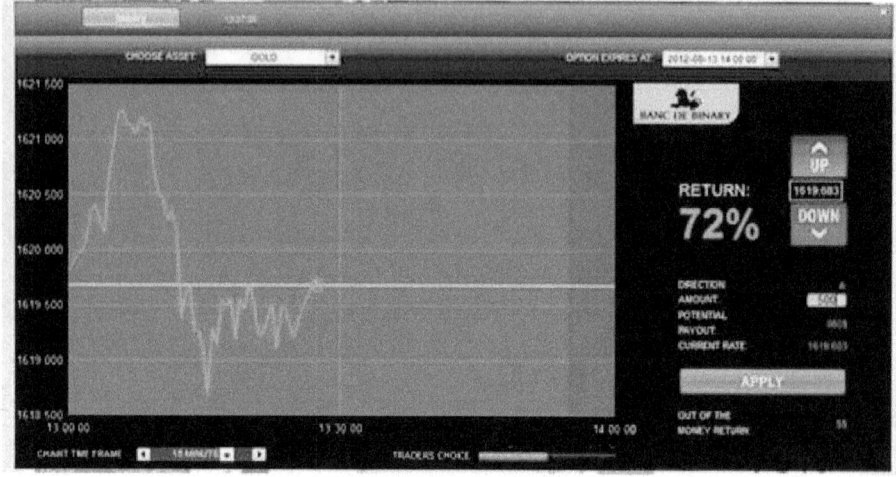

Screenshot of a Binary Trading Interface – Choose Up Or Down, How Much To Risk and "Apply".

Up or Down aka 'Call or Put.'

Do you think the price of "x" is going up or down? In the screenshot above from Banc De Binary, we are looking at the current price of gold. Gold is "x". The green line is the price movement of the gold over the course of time. The red section on the right-hand side is the last moment you can trade this binary option. After that point, the option is closed for trading. It has not expired quite yet if you traded previously, however your window of trading is over.

If you think the price of "Gold" is going up you place a "call".

If you think the price of "Gold" is going down, you place a "put".

Those are your only two options. Hence "Binary". If you pick the right choice of the two you win the trade. If you pick wrong, you lose the trade. There are two choices only. 'Up or Down.' And two outcomes, 'Win or Lose'.

That is the very basics of binary trading for dummies. It is that simple, and it is designed to be that easy. Your return is clearly stated before hitting the 'apply' button. You will earn 72% on your investment if you finish the trade 'in the money'.

"X" can be any number of underlying assets. It can be a certain stock or it can be the price of gold or oil. It can be a currency pair or it can be the price of facebooks stock. You get to choose what underlying asset you want to trade.

There is one more important factor left out of the simple illustration above and that is the expiration time or maturity date of the option. This is the point in time when the trade expires. This is the point when the actual price of the underlying asset is determined and you find out if you finished the trade 'in the money' with a win, or 'out of the money' with a loss.

If you chose 'up, or call' and at the price expired higher, you win. The expiration times vary from as fast as 60 seconds to as long as hours, days and even weeks.

Example Basic Binary Trade

The easiest way to explain what a binary trade looks like is to provide an example.

Example Trade 1 – Trading Googles Stock With A High / Low Binary Option

Screenshot From Google Finance of Current Price Of Google

Perhaps Google is doing well and you expect it to be trading above $672.10 by 3:30pm est this afternoon. A binary trade means you place a bet on that theory

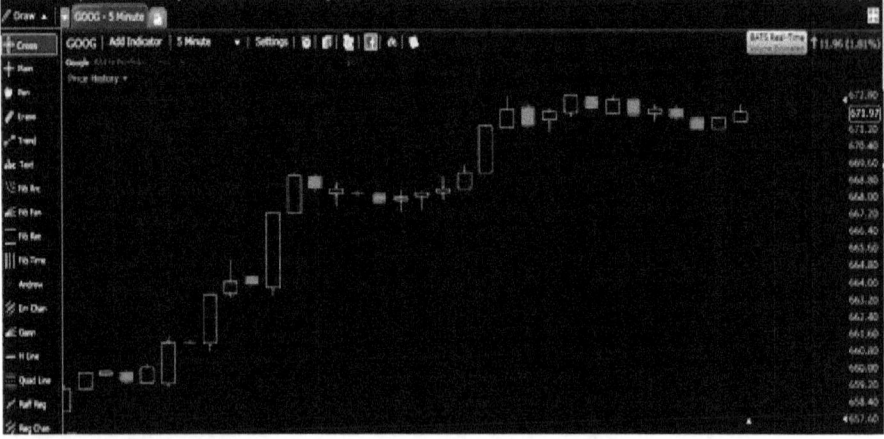

Corresponding Candlestick Chart From FreeStockCharts.com For Google's Stock Price.

Above is the corresponding candlestick chart for Google, from FreeStockCharts.com. You can use this to read price action and find trading opportunities.

Here is the Corresponding Trade From TradeRush.com – Risk of $1000, Return of $1700 If You Win – $100 Rebate If you Lose (10%)

And here is the corresponding Binary trade offered by TradeRush.com – You risk $1000.00 that Google's stock will be trading at or above $672.10 at 3:30pm later today. Your return on this trade is 70% if you win and 10% if you lose.

When 3:30pm rolls around and Google's stock is trading at or above $672.1.00 as you predicted, you'll be paid $1700.00. This includes your $1000 you put up on the trade up front and the 70% return ($700).

If you're wrong and the stock is trading at less than $672.10, you receive $100, a 10% rebate, losing $900 total (Your $1000 investment amount minus the $100 return = $900 loss).

In the example above, $672.10 is called the "strike price." Since you bet in a positive direction, we would refer to this as a "call," not a "put." $700.00 is the "payoff value." The date and time are called the "expiration date," or the maturity date. The $100 is the losing return, or a 10% rebate offered sometimes on trades. Not all binary options brokers offer rebates on trades that finish out of the money.

You could also have a bet in the opposite direction, that the stock's price would be trading at or below a certain lower value, which would have been a "put." In that situation, you would need google to finish below the strike price. Usually, this would be a few pips below what the strike price would be if it was a call. This price is set by the individual broker along with the returns offered. It is up to the trader to take the trade or not.

Example 2 – Tutorial on Trading The Price Of Gold With A 'Touch Trade

If you want to profit from the swings in the gold market, there are hardly any better ways to do so than with a binary option. With a one touch trade, the only thing that has to happen for you to win is that the asset should hit the 1 touch price.

You bet $100 that the price of gold will touch $1617.40 by 3pm EST today.

The payout for this trade is 70% if you finish in the money. If you win, you will get a payout of $170 which includes your $100 risked up front plus the $70 return (70% of $100 = $70). Since a 70% return is a bit low on the payout side, the broker offers a 15% rebate on losses. If you lose, you get $15 back and only lose $85 instead of the full $100.

You can see how this can offset the lower than average return for wins.

You place the trade and need the price of gold to reach the target price, or trigger price of $1617.40 before 3pm today.

Luckily for you, there was some negative news regarding the dollar's value that drove fears of inflation. The price of gold and oil went up accordingly. When the news broke, the gold price spiked up and hit your target price. Triggering your trade to close in the money. You were paid $170 which includes your $100 bet up front plus the $70 return on your investment. You can trade one touch options at sites like 24option.com, not all brokers offer them even though they are the 2nd most popular form of binary trading.

A General Trading Example

Trade commodities like gold and oil with easy to buy binary options. Choose your underlying asset. IE gold, currency pair, stock etc.

Decide how long until you want the option to expire. As little as 60 seconds and as up as days or weeks. Common expiry times are 15-30 minutes.

Choose the amount you wish to risk. As little as $5, as much as thousands.

Decide which way you think the price is going to move (up or down).

Click "Up or Down" and hit the "Apply" Button – just before hitting "Apply" you will see the exact payout if you win or lose.

At expiry you have either won or lost and get the fixed payout offered prior to hitting the 'apply' button.

You can not lose more than your risked amount and you can not make more than your fixed return, regardless of how far the price moves.

Binaries are one or the other choice with a one or the other payout or loss. Winning returns average 70-85% at the respectable brokers for most trades. If you lose, you get between 0-15%. Some brokers kick back some percentages on losses, that's why their winning returns are sometimes a bit lower compared to the other brokers.

Things To Remember Before You Begin Making Option Trades

The risk is known up front and fixed. You can not lose more than you put into any trade.

You are not and can not get burned by leverage like you can with forex trading.

You do not need to set 'stop losses'. The return is the same whether you win or lose by 1 pip or 100 pips.

Payouts are clearly stated and known exactly up front before risking any money on the trade.

Most of the brokers we list have early closure feature. This lets you close your option at a price they are offering any time up until the final closing minutes. You can lock in profit or minimize loss with early exit

Executing the trade is easy. Choose your asset to trade, how much to risk, choose 'up or down' and click the 'trade now' button.

- Returns are 70-85% on average at the trading brokers listed here.
- No hidden costs – Your risk and full return are clearly listed.
- You do not have to be a financial "expert" to win.
- You never take any actual ownership of the underlying asset. You are just predicting what happens to the price of the asset.
- Your trade comes down to a 'one or the other' choice (hence binary)
- The trading is simple by design

Chapter 2: Getting Started

If you know what a binary option is but would like to learn how to get started with trading binaries then jump back over to our page focused on the things you need to know to start trading. This page is more of a basic overview of what is going on when talking about binary options.

Trading Binary Options For Dummies

Anyone can trade binary options. Even a dummy can win any given binary trade, too. It is one or the other choice, it is hard to get it that wrong all of the time.

However, to be a long term winner you have to develop a method and strategy that works for you. You have to consistently profit by winning more trades than you lose. Since there is risk involved, it means that you need to create a method to succeed. You can do that by studying up on our tips and strategies to win and practicing with a no risk trading account. We also recommend learning the basics of candlestick chart reading in order to judge price action.

If you are ready to take the next steps and learn more about binary trading then jump back to our Binary Trading Guide list of lessons and continue reading through the lessons and tutorials. You certainly want to learn to read a candlestick chart as well as find the right broker to trade with.

Classified as exotic options, binary options is a type of financial derivative that offers traders a fixed return on their investment. While in essence, binary options only have 2 possible outcomes, most binary options brokers nowadays offer traders several varieties in the ways they can trade binary options. The most popular of these is the classic High/Low (Call/Put) option.

It is important that the trader understands all the risks involved in trading this often misunderstood financial instrument

What makes binary options truly attractive to traders is their simplicity. An investor in binary options only has 2 main factors to worry about; the direction of the price movement and the expiry time. If the investor is able to determine the right direction of the price movement and the ideal expiry time for the option to close on the right side of the trade, then his investment will close in the money.

Unlike traditional or vanilla options, the quantum of the price movement for binary options is irrelevant and has no effect on the amount of the payoff. Nevertheless, while binary options offer a simplistic way to trade the dynamic financial markets, it is important that the trader understands all the risks involved in trading this often misunderstood financial instrument.

Are Binary options trading gambling?

Many articles have been written about binary options, often evaluating binary options trading to gambling. This is largely due to the fact that many people misunderstand the simplicity of binary options as being nothing more than glamorized gambling. The fact is, this is far from true. Before their debut to the retail trading sector in 2008, binary options had actually been around for decades.

They were initially used by the insurance industry to help insurance companies quantify insurance risks especially against catastrophic events such as storms or earthquakes. In fact, without binary options, many people today would not have been able to insure their homes from damages caused by natural disasters.

Of course, there is also a tendency for some people to get carried away with binary options due to how simple it is to trade them. And when these people lose all their money, they tell themselves that it is gambling to justify their losses. The fact is, binary options trading is like any other forms of financial trading. If you do not know what you are trading then chances are you are going to lose all your money.

This is why it is essential that you educate yourself properly regarding the markets and assets that you are going to invest in. Educating yourself in the financial market doesn't just entail reading the financial news but also understanding how the markets work and how each piece of news can affect their movements. In addition, you need to also learn how to trade the various markets using the proper trading strategies. With the right amount of trading education, you will begin to see more clearly on how you can use binary options strategically to benefit monetarily

Benefits of binary options

Although spot forex trading has been around for much longer than binary options trading, binary options trading have several distinct advantages over the former.

- First of all, with binary options trading, there is no leverage trading available. This means binary traders have better control over their trading risks than spot forex traders.
- With binary options, you cannot lose more than what you invested unlike when you trade on margin. With binary options trading, you also know beforehand how much you will be getting in return which makes it easier for you to calculate your risk/reward ratio.
- Another benefit of binary options trading is the faster turnaround time. Comparatively, binary options trades are executed over a much shorter term than traditional financial trading. And because of the shorter turnaround

time, binary traders can profit substantially more with their limited investment capital than forex or stock traders.
- Finally, the average returns offered by binary options brokers ranges from 70% to 85% which is quite lucrative when we compared to what most investors earn from traditional investments. Given all the above-mentioned benefits, it is easy to see why binary options trading is becoming ever more popular.

Trading Binary Options

Apart from being simple to trade, binary options traders have a wide range of instruments that they can trade in. Nowadays, most brokers are able to offer traders binary options for currency pairs, commodities, stocks and market indices. In some cases, there are also binary options for bonds.

In order to look at the simplicity of this trade type let's look at an example; let's say you want to trade in forex binary options, the EUR/USD specifically

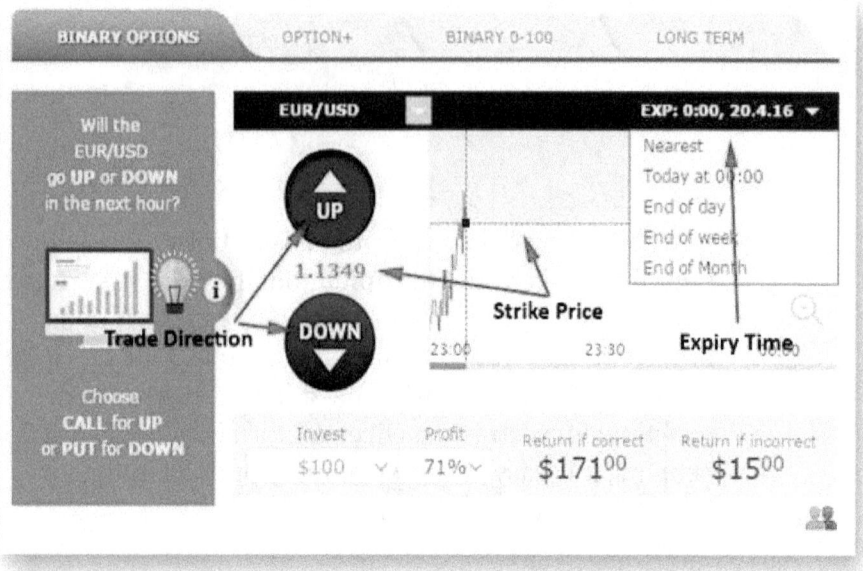

Using the screenshot above as a reference, you first determine if the EUR/USD is going to end up higher or lower (trade direction) than the strike price of 1.1349. Next, select the expiry time for the option which will correspond to what you predicted.

From the above example, you can choose the expiration time of 60 minutes (00:00), end of the day, end of week or end of the month. Once you have determined both the direction as well as the expiry time, decide how much you want to invest and after that just wait for the option to expire. If your option closes in the money, you will earn a profit of $71. And if your trade closes out of the money, the broker, in this case, Anyoption, will refund 15% of what you invested.

How do Binaries Work?

In their simplest form, binary options can go only one of two directions, hence their name. You can be right or you can be wrong. They are an all or nothing type of trade and there is no middle ground. This might sound threatening, but they really are easy to understand. You select an asset and then predict whether you think that the asset will go up or down in price. Once you figure this out, the broker that you are working with will display the percentage amount that you will have returned to you prior to officially committing your money to the trade. You then select the amount that you want to risk and the timeframe with which you want to work within. Once these basic factors are all accounted for, you will click on the button that executes the trade.

This is one of the greatest things about binary options. You have more information about how the trade will conclude with this type of trading than with any other type of trading. You know exactly how much you stand to gain and exactly at what time that money will appear. Binaries lay all of these things out prior to your commitment.

Trading Tip – Make sure your computer is working in an optimal state

What Can You Trade?

With binary options, you can trade all of the major currency pairs, stocks, indices, and commodities. The exciting thing is that you are not limited to any one place. Whether you want to trade gold futures, Apple's stock, or the Japanese yen, you can do it all from the same platform. You can also trade on an international scale without having to change brokers. Many of the top brokers include numerous stocks and indices from Europe and Asia, allowing international traders to use their platforms without a problem. The good news for you is that brokers act as a one-stop shopping place for all of your trading desires. You can trade pretty much everything with the same website without having to keep switching screens.

How Long Do Trades Last?

With binary options, it's important to remember that all of your trades will have strict timelines that you need to pay attention to. Some of these can be pretty short or they can last a bit longer. Ultimately, you will need to decide what time frames work best for you. If you don't like having money tied up in a trade for a long time, 60 second or 5-minute options might be best for you. If you don't mind waiting, you can trade hour long trades or longer.

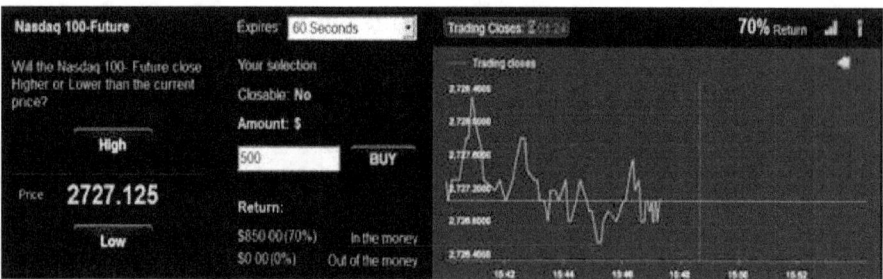

The thing to remember about expiry times is that they are adaptable only up until you commit to the trade. Once the trade is locked in, you need to sit back and wait. This is different from other types of trading where you can sell off your purchase shares at any time you want, but it is a fact of options trading that you cannot get around. Some brokers will allow you to sell off your trade for a small refund, but this is a rare scenario that you shouldn't worry about until you become an advanced trader.

Main Types of Options

There are three main types of binary options that you need to be aware of. The first is the basic call/put trade. Here you are simply attempting to predict whether the price of the asset will have gone up or down at the time of expiration.

The next type of trade is the one touch trade. Here, you will be given a target price at the beginning of the trade. If the asset reaches that price or beyond at any time during the life of the trade, your investment will be deemed a profitable one. This price is always stipulated by the broker before you execute the trade so you can best prepare your information ahead of time.

The last of the three major types is the boundary trade. With this choice, the broker will give you a range of prices and it is up to you to determine whether the price of the asset will be within or outside the given range.

Percentage Payouts

There are a few different variations of these trades, and some of the more exotic versions can have pretty high payouts, some around 300 percent, depending on the broker. One example is a one touch trade with a really far off target price. Usually, in order to get the big payouts on these, you need to go with the hardest to reach option. For this example, you would have to select that yes, the far off target price will be attained. These have higher rates of return because they are much harder to be correct upon.

Which Binary Option is Best for Me?

Figuring out which choice is going to be best for you is something that will be different for each person. First, you want to look at where your experience lay. Are you a former Forex trader looking to augment profits with a new strategy? If this is the case, your expertise on the currency market is fully transferable to the binary options marketplace. Or maybe you are a former day trader, looking to alleviate some of your risks. If this is true, binary options can certainly help, and you will want, to begin with, focus on the stocks that you are most familiar with.

Ultimately it comes down to what your goals are. You need to figure out what your trading goals might be and then develop a plan to realize those goals. If you want to make $1,000 per week, you need to figure out which types of options will help you to hit this mark, and which timeframes will be best suited to get you there. The answer to the above question is something that will be different for each person, but you should always place an emphasis on the quality of your trading and not on the quantity. Five trades per day that are correct are going to return more to you than six correct and four incorrect

Where do I Start?

First, you need to select a broker. Once you've figured out which broker will best suit your needs, you deposit your trading money with them via a credit card or wire transfer. Make sure that your trading money is money that you can afford to lose and not funds that you will need to get through your daily life.

Start Trading

Once you have created an account and have funded it, you are set to begin trading. But you shouldn't start right away. Many brokers now have demo trading accounts, and you need to take full advantage of these if you can. Demo trading is basically no-risk trading. You are given play money and for a limited time you are able to trade those play dollars in real time and learn the ropes of how binary options work. The longer you demo trade, the smaller the learning curve will be when you start trading with your own real money. Even if you only have 72 hours to demo trade, you need to capitalize on this. At the very least, you want to learn the software that you will be using in order to eliminate the possibility of user error.

Demo trading should be used as much as possible until you have established a strategy that works for you and you are confident with it. You want to eliminate the possibility of mistake because of inexperience. You want to use them as much as possible while you have the opportunity available to you.

Chapter 3: Key Concepts for Beginners

Entering the world of binary options can be a daunting experience for beginners. Everywhere you turn there's a new word, such as "spot price" or "out of the money" for you to get your head around. You might think that you need to be a stock market trader in order to understand the world of binary options. Not true! In this installment of our Binary Options Guide, we'll break the binary options world into its key components and explain how each part works. By the time you've finished reading, you'll feel more prepared to tackle the diverse and fast-paced world of binary options trading. We shall be focusing on the following under listed points

- Binary Option
- Broker
- What Does a Binary Option Look Like?
- Rise/Fall
- Asset
- Spot Price
- Price of the Option
- Time Frame
- Entry Spot/Exit Spot
- In the Money/Out of the Money/At the Money
- Early Exit and Extension
- Payout and Profit
- Odds and Probability
- Conclusion

Binary Option

You may already know what binary options are, especially if you've read our introductory article. But here's a reminder. With every binary options trade, you're trying to predict what will happen to the price of an asset (e.g. gold or shares in a company) within a given time frame.

Signpost With Yes And No Options In Green And Red Binary options are usually framed in terms of a question with a yes or no answer. For instance, will the Tesco share price rise within the next 15 minutes? There are two possibilities – yes or no. If your choice turns out to be correct, you'll win a predetermined return. If you're wrong, you'll lose what you staked.

The word trade is used very loosely in the binary options world. People talk about trading binary options, purchasing binary options and betting on binary options. You can use whichever phrase you prefer. They all relate to the same question – what's going to happen to the price of an asset in the future?

Broker

Binary Dot Com Logo

Logo of the broker, Binary.com

To trade or gamble with binary options, you're going to need an online broker. Binary options brokers provide an electronic platform for betting/trading to take place. Examples include:

- Binary.com
- AnyOption.com
- 24Option.com
- BancDeBinary.com

A binary broker is a bit like a bookmaker; however, instead of offering bets and odds related to horses, they offer bets and odds related to the prices of assets.

Each broker uses trading software that automatically churns out data related to particular bets, such as a bet's "return", "profit" and "price". The figures quoted by brokers are constantly changing and being re-calculated by their software, as the price of each asset moves. We'll discuss what these figures mean later.

Some brokers request that you download their trading software to make trades, whereas others will allow you to use it from their website.

Signing up for an account with a broker is usually free and straightforward. Some will allow you to open demo accounts, which enable you to practice trading with pretend money. We'll explain how to set up a demo account in a future article, so look out for that.

What Does a Binary Option Look Like?

In Figure 1 (below) you'll see a screenshot of a binary options trade from Binary.com, with key features labeled. Binary.com is a well-respected broker that's regulated by the UK gambling commission and has been around for 15 years. It was first established under the name BetOnMarkets.com in 2000. We'll be referring back to this screenshot, throughout the article.

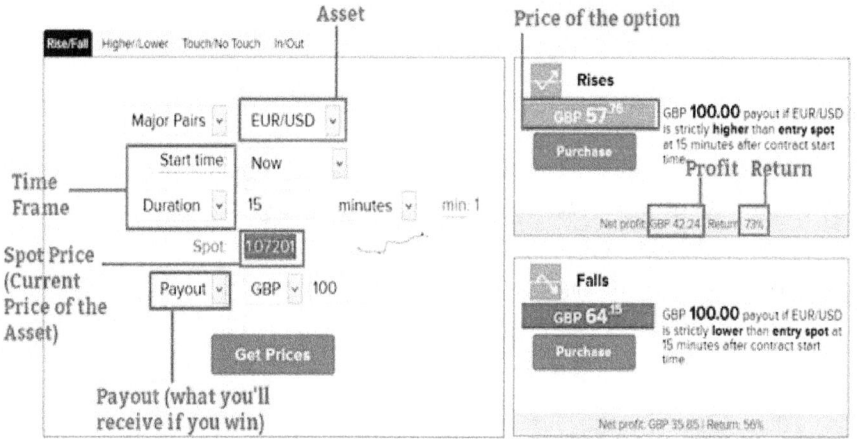

Rise/Fall

As you can see at the top left of Figure 1, Rise/Fall is selected. Rise/Fall is the most common type of binary option and is also known as the High/Low option or Up/Down option. It involves answering the question – will the price of this asset be higher or lower than its current price, after a specified period of time (e.g. 15 minutes)? We'll discuss other types of binary option in a future article: Types of Trade.

Asset

Pile of Gold Bars

ASSET

An asset is simply a resource of economic value. Examples of assets include gold, oil, shares in a company and currency pairs. The asset shown in Figure 1 is the currency pair – EUR/USD. To read more about assets, look out for our future article: What are Assets?

Spot Price

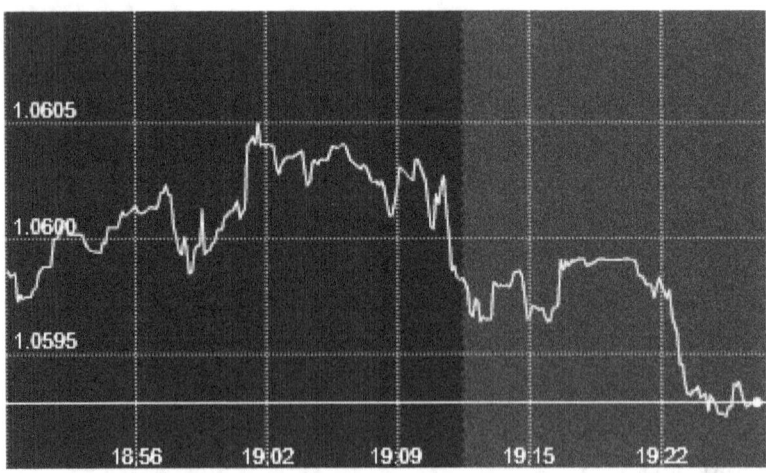

Graph Showing Price Over Time For EUR/USD

Graph showing price movement over time for Eur/USD

The Spot Price is the current price of your chosen asset. Spot Prices are constantly changing, and trying to predict what this price will be in the future is what binary options betting is all about.

Price of the Option

Once you've chosen which option you want to purchase (or which bet you want to place) you pay the price of the option to your broker. The price of the Rise option, in Figure 1, is quoted as £57.76, and the price of the Fall option is £64.15. As you'll see, when we discuss probability later in the article, the price of the option is directly related to the probability of the option being successful.

The price you pay for the option will be your maximum potential loss for your bet. In other words, if your bet is unsuccessful, you won't lose any more than the sum you paid for the option. With some brokers, you may receive a small refund, if your bet is unsuccessful. So, it's not necessarily an all-or-nothing situation. For instance, at AnyOption.com, you'll receive a refund of between 5 – 25 % of the price of your option, if you lose.

TIMEFRAME

Time is a key concept in binary options trading, as when you're trying to predict whether an asset's price will rise or fall, it's always with respect to a particular time frame.

At Binary.com you'll be allowed to choose the start and end of your time frame. (Most of the other binary brokers will only let you choose the end time). The time-frame could be anything between 10 seconds and 365 days.

Being able to choose the start of your bet is a very useful function as it can allow you to take advantage of influential events in the wider world. For instance, if you know that a successful technology manufacturer is due to release a new product tomorrow afternoon, you might choose to bet on the share price of that manufacturer rising tomorrow afternoon.

Entry Spot/Exit Spot

To determine whether your bet has been successful, the spot price at the start of your time window – which is sometimes called the entry spot – will be compared with the spot price at the end of the time window – which is sometimes called the exit spot.

For instance, suppose we purchased the Rise option for EUR/USD, and we chose to frame our bet from now until 15 minutes in the future – which is what we've selected in Figure 1.

For our Rise option bet to be successful, the exit spot would have to be higher than the entry spot in 15 minutes time. If we selected the Fall option, to be successful our exit spot would have to be lower than our entry spot in 15 minutes time.

In the Money/Out of the Money/At the Money

> In the Money = Successful Bet
>
> Out of the Money
>   = Unsuccessful Bet
>
> At the Money = It's a draw!

Blackboard Cartoon With Definitions For In The Money/At The Money/Out Of The Money.

If your bet is successful it's sometimes described as being in the money. When your bet is unsuccessful, you're out of the money.

There's a 3rd possibility. What happens if the exit spot is exactly the same as the entry spot? Brokers sometimes describe this situation as being at the money. Brokers will have a particular policy that they'll refer to if you end up "at the money". Make sure you check what your broker's policy is for "at the money" options before placing a bet.

Early Exit and Extension

Certain brokers – including binary.com – allow early exits. An early exit is when you exit your bet before your pre-specified time for a reduced percentage return. This is a useful option if you find that the market has taken a sudden turn for the worse, and you want to lower your chances of finishing "out of the money".

Some brokers – such as Banc de Binary – allow trades (or bets) to be extended. At Banc de Binary you can do this up until 10 minutes before expiry. This function is useful if the price of your asset is moving slower than you thought it would, and you want a bit more time to see if it will make a profit.

Payout and Profit

Stick Figure Holding Bills With Sack Of Money

You need to select your payout – this is the amount of money you'll receive if you win. In Figure 1, we've selected a payout of £100. Payouts could range from £1 to £100 000, depending on the broker. Your payout includes the price of the option, and you can work out the profit you'll make by subtracting the price of the option from your total payout.

Take a look at the blackboard below to see how the profit is calculated for bets related to the Rise and Fall options

Odds and Probability

When you calculate the odds and probability of some event taking place, you're using two instruments that gauge how likely it is that an event is going to happen. Knowing this information will help you assess the level of risk associated with placing certain bets. In this section, we'll show you that...

The price of the option is directly related to the probability that the bet will be successful

The percentage return is directly related to the odds that it will be successful

Calculating Odds

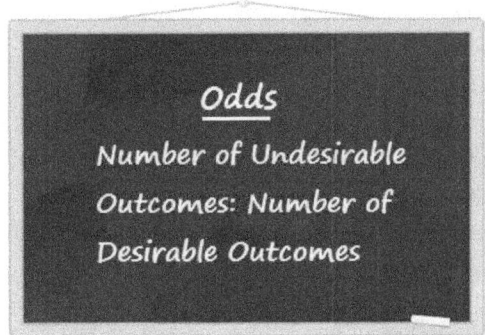

Blackboard Cartoon With How To Calculate Odds Written On It. Odds are calculated by comparing the number of undesirable outcomes with the number of desirable outcomes.

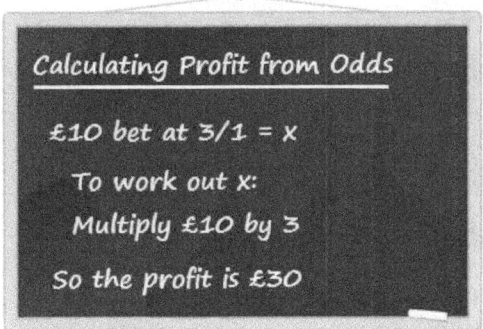

For example, let's suppose you wanted to work out the odds of throwing a six on your next dice roll. We know that there's 1 desirable outcome (rolling a 6) and 5 undesirable ones (rolling a 1, rolling a 2 and so on). We would express the odds of rolling a six as 6/1.

In gambling, you can use odds to calculate what your profit will be, as odds tell you how much money you can make from a stake of 1 unit. Suppose you want to bet on a horse with odds of 3/1. These odds tell you that, if your bet is successful, for every unit you stake, that unit will be multiplied by 3.

What are the odds for our binary bets? Let's consider the Rise option first. We know what our profit for this bet would be £42.24. We also know that the number of desirable outcomes is 1 (that the price will rise). But we don't know how this compares to the number of undesirable outcomes, which we'll represent as x.

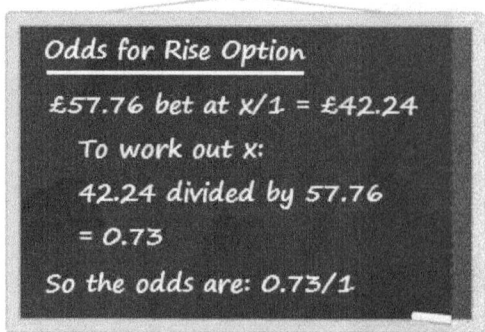

Simply convert the figure of 0.73 to a percentage (multiply by 100) to arrive at the figure of your return: 73%. You can see that the return directly reflects the odds (see Figure 1).

While we're at it, let's work out the odds for the Fall bet too. We know that the price of the option is £64.15 and that the profit will be £35.85. When it comes to the odds, we know that there's one desired outcome (that the price falls), but how many undesirable outcomes are there (x)?

```
Odds for Fall Option
£64.15 bet at x/1 = £35.85
    To work out x:
    35.85 divided by 64.15
    = 0.56
So the odds are: 0.56/1
```

When you convert 0.56 to a percentage (i.e. multiply by 100) you get 56%, which is the figure that is quoted as your return (see Figure 1).

Calculating probability from odds

Probability is similar to odds in that it's another way of measuring the likelihood of an event taking place. However, instead of simply comparing the number of undesirable outcomes with the number of desirable outcomes, you'll be comparing the number of desirable outcomes with the sum of all possible outcomes. This sounds confusing, but don't worry. You'll see what we mean in a moment.

Here's the sum we use to calculate probability using odds:

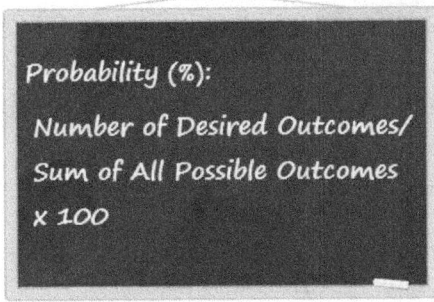

```
Probability (%):
Number of Desired Outcomes/
Sum of All Possible Outcomes
x 100
```

To calculate the 'sum of all possible outcomes' simply add the 'number of desired outcomes' (1) to the 'number of undesired outcomes' (0.73). You'll see that we've done this in the blackboard below:

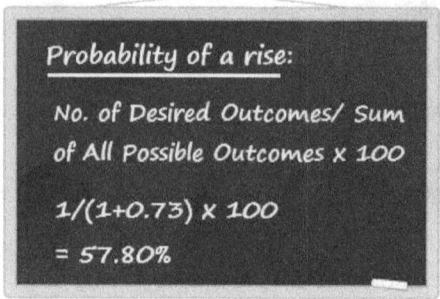

So, the Rise Option has a 57.80% chance of coming off. As you can see this figure directly reflects the price of the option, which is £57.76 (see Figure 1). Don't worry about the fact that there's a 0.04 difference between the two figures. Binary.com have simply rounded their figure up.

What about the Fall Option?

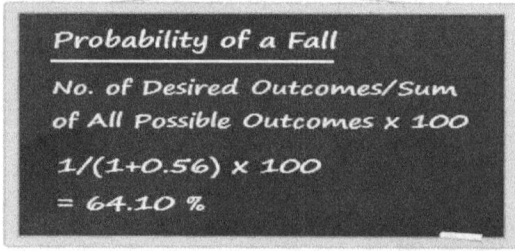

The possibility of the Fall option being successful is 64.10%, which is directly related to the price of the option: £64.15 (see Figure 1). There's a 0.05 difference between these figures which is related to rounding.

The results of our calculations tell us that the Fall option is somewhat more likely to be successful than the Rise option. But there's not a huge difference – only 6.39%. To use a horse-racing analogy, there isn't a clear favorite between these two options. To make a more informed decision, we'd need to do a bit more research into the asset we're betting on. Look out for our articles on Technical Analysis and Fundamental Analysis in which we'll show you the tools you can use to research an asset's price movement.

In conclusion, by grasping key concepts such as "spot price", "profit", "return", "odds" and "probability", you'll be in a much better position to trade wisely. Remember, however, that understanding the figures quoted by binary brokers is not the whole story. Consider horse racing. Some people make decisions about which horse to bet on simply by looking at the odds. But experienced horse race gamblers take other things into account, such as the track record of each horse, and the weather on the day of the race. You can do the same thing with binary options.

Chapter 4: Binary Options Strategies

Earlier, we mentioned about trading binary options with a proper trading strategy. This is an area which most new traders tend to neglect as they are anxious to jump right into trading binary options. This is also the main reason why new traders tend to lose all their initial trading capital as they do not know what they are really doing.

Having a proper trading strategy is important as the strategy helps to keep you on track with your trade. Can you imagine driving a car without a proper destination? So why should you risk your money without having a clear direction on how to trade?

Developing a trading strategy is not difficult once you understand the market analysis that goes into a developing one. A good trading strategy should encompass both fundamental and technical analysis. This is to ensure that you cover all the avenues and not overlook anything that might affect the price movements. Tools such as price charts and technical indicators are all there to help get a clearer picture of how the market is behaving as well as how it is going to behave in the future. Trending markets and ranging markets all call for different trading strategies and in order to come out ahead, you need to know what kind of trading strategy you can employ.

Binary Options Analysis Methods/Techniques

You will learn about the following concepts:

- Why is analysis key to success
- Fundamental analysis
- Technical analysis
- Types of technical analysis

- Chart patterns
- Reversal bar patterns

As we have already pointed out numerous times throughout our guide, the analysis is crucial for success no matter what you are trading. Although many people liken binary options to gaming, it is exactly analysis, both technical and fundamental, that skews the odds in your favor to above 50% (given we assume that the price has a 50% to go up or down from the spot price). Without a proper assessment of the market conditions, however, binary options trading is nothing more than simple betting which leaves you exposed to the factor of luck, and we know that luck is only temporary.

The current article will explain the basics of technical and fundamental analysis but will not dive into specifics as we have already thoroughly explained most fundamental and technical factors which tend to influence an asset's pricing. Because binary options are basically bets on an asset's price movement, analysis means used for the Forex, stock and commodities market apply to trading binary options

Fundamental analysis

Fundamental analysis refers to a methodology of predicting an asset's price fluctuations and future trends based on external factors such as economic data, central bank decisions and comments, political and geopolitical events, force majeure occurrences and so on. All of this information is crucial for binary trading because it affects market sentiment, and market sentiment is what moves the markets.

For many traders, and especially in academic studies, fundamental analysis is considered as the primary assessment and prediction methodology for an asset's price movement. And although technical analysis has been increasingly gaining in popularity, especially with the development of modern day technology, the impact of fundamental factors forces many technicians, who usually don't take into account news, economic indicators etc., to avoid trading during the time of their releases.

Fundamental analysis basically includes every factor from the real world that can affect the pricing of a certain asset. For example, the EUR/USD pair is influenced by economic data coming out from the Eurozone and the United States, central bank decisions, central bankers' comments and so on. Commodities, such as oil and copper, for example, tend to fluctuate widely when economic data shows a change in demand prospects, especially in major consumers, or by any outages in supply. When it comes to stocks, they are influenced not only by the overall economic outlook but also by company-specific information, such as corporate news, earnings reports, and performance forecasts.

Economic calendar

Calendar-icon (1)

One of the main sources of fundamental information used on a daily basis is the economic calendar. Depending on the calendar's thoroughness, it can include all of the low, medium and high-volatility indicators from a certain economy. Thus, economic calendars provide you with a comprehensive and auto-updated overview of a certain economy's performance.

Logically, high-volatility indicators are the most closely watched, especially the ones released by the world's top economies. Among these data are unemployment numbers, GDP growth rate, inflation, retail sales, consumer sentiment, industrial production, manufacturing and services Purchasing, Managers' Index and so on. Read through our Forex Trading Academy's "Fundamental

Analysis" section to gain a more in-depth understanding of the indicators and force majeure events of utmost significance.

Technical analysis

Technical analysis is the second main line of study used to evaluate securities and their expected fluctuations. Technical analysis is based on three pillars: every event and piece of information are already factored in the asset's price; once a trend has been established, it will likely continue; everything is bound to repeat and traders react in a similar way of repeating market occurrences. Technical analysis is based entirely on historic market data.

This is why technicians (traders practicing technical analysis) spend most of their time looking for the formation of distinct price patterns on the chart, which they expect will be followed by a well-known price movement.

Technicians typically disregard fundamental factors, even the most significant ones. At first, you might think that this seems illogical and wrong, but there is a good reason for it – you are completely unaffected by the bombardment of news and comments by "experts".

However, as we said above, fundamental analysis's capability to move the markets is too overwhelming to be ignored. This is why many technicians, especially day traders, often close their positions and abstain from entering the markets before, during and shortly after major economic data is released as it can completely override their expectations from the technical point of view and gun their stop-loss orders. Learn more on the matter by reading through our Forex Academy's "Technical Analysis" section. Additionally, if you want to learn more about day trading, check out our "Day Trading" guide.

Types of technical analysis

Generally speaking, there are two main trading styles technicians adopt – trading based on strategies incorporating the great variety of technical indicators (such as Relative Strength Index, Moving Average Convergence Divergence, Stochastic Oscillator etc), and price action trading.

Chart patterns, bar reversal patterns

Regardless of the trading type, you wish to choose, chart patterns are the core of the technical analysis. While reading up on both price action trading and trading via technical indicators, you will constantly encounter the terms "channel", "triangle", "wedge", "flag", "pennant" and so on. These formations, which we have covered in our "Forex Trading Academy" and "Price Action Trading Academy" guides, are plotted by the market's movement as it displays certain behavior. Up-down arrows. However, the market sooner or later shifts its behavior. It is inevitable. And because technical traders believe that the market almost always acts in a manner similar to past experience, they wait for such a pattern to occur on their charts in order to gain an idea of what might happen next and enter an appropriate position. For example, patterns most often end with a breakout in one of the two possible directions, and so traders guess which one it will be. Also, some patterns are typical reversal scenarios, while others generally tend to resume the market's previous direction of movement (such as flags and pennants).

Apart from the larger chart patterns, which may take up to 40-50 bars (candlesticks) before being completed, there are also small reversal bar patterns. They consist of one, two or three bars and illustrate a price reversal, as you can judge by their name. Traders observe these patterns in order to determine whether the reversal will have a follow-through or will fake out. To learn more about reversal bar patterns, check out our articles "Bars Signaling Reversal – Basic Features", "Further Talk on Reversal Bars", "Reversal Bars – Examples", "Two-Bar Reversals", "Three-Bar Reversals", "Outside Bars" and "Other Types of Signal Bars and Patterns".

LEARN HOW TO USE CHARTS

Basics

Binary options derive their value from an underlying asset. Therefore you don't need to use your binary options broker's trading platform to analyze charts of that underlying asset. You can analyze the underlying asset directly–with more customizability and more trading tools–utilizing the charts on this site. If you are trading binary options in the EUR/USD, you'll want to pull up a chart of the EUR/USD and use the tools available on our site to make better trading decisions.

If you are trading a stock binary option, input the stock symbol to see how the stock is moving now and how it has moved in the past.

Pick Your Asset

Input the asset (either name or symbol) you are trading into the box on the upper left

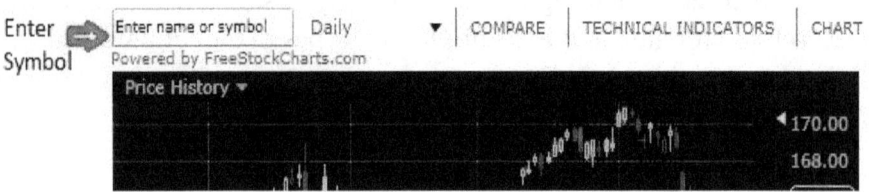

As you start typing a drop-down list appears making it very easy to find the asset you are looking for.

Pick Your Time Frame

Next to the symbol box is a drop down menu. By default, this setting is "Daily". This will show the daily price history of your asset. Each bar you see represents one day, and therefore it is a good time frame to see the overall price direction of an asset's price.

For day trading purposes, or trading short-term binary options, you'll also want to see how the asset's price has performed over a short-term timeframe. By selecting a shorter time frame, such as a 1 minute, 5 minute or 15 minute chart, you are zooming to see how the price is performing right now.

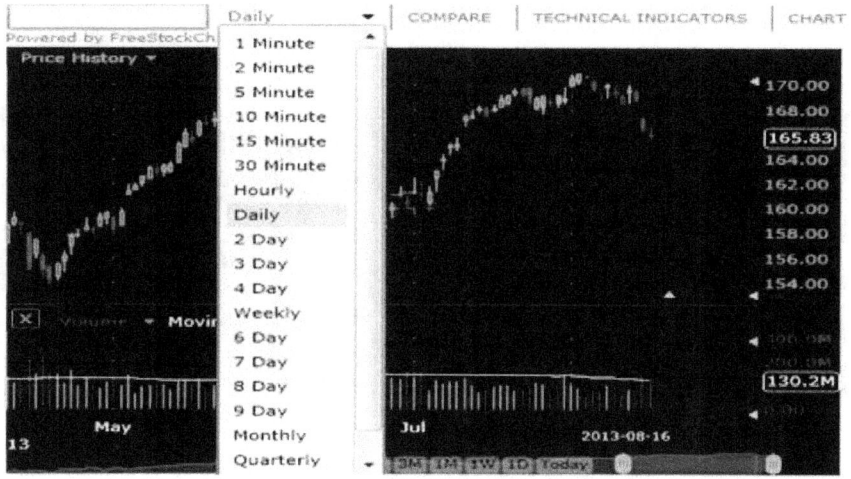

If you select "5 Minute" then each bar on the chart will reflect 5 minutes of price data.

Compare Tool

The Compare tool is great if you want to see two or more assets side by side. By seeing the price charts of multiple assets side by side, you can potentially determine which ones are relatively weak and which ones are relatively strong; this can help you determine which assets you wish to buy puts or calls in.

After clicking "Compare," input symbols you want to compare to the asset already on the chart.

Here is a daily chart of the EUR/USD and I have compared it to the GBP/USD (blue line).

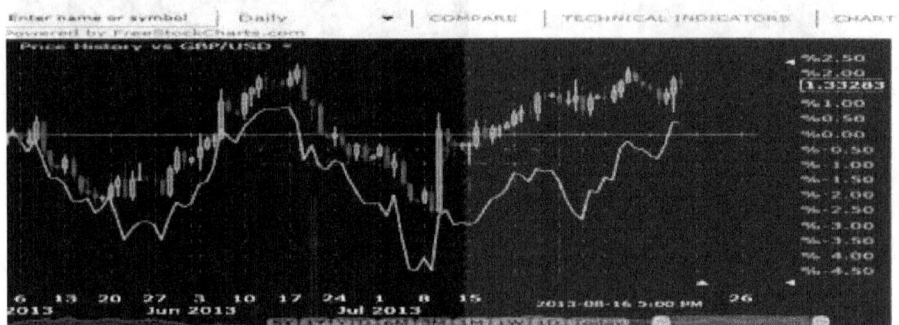

The scale along the right is a percentage, not a dollar amount since the assets are different prices. The percentage scale allows you to see which asset(s) is stronger or weaker in terms of percentage movements.

If you don't like the percentage scale, you can turn it off by deselecting the "Show Percentage Scale" in the Compare tool.

To quit comparing, go back into Compare and deselect (uncheck) or delete the assets from your compare list.

Technical Indicators

Free Binary Options Charts offers you over 60 indicators to choose from. Simply click on "Technical Indicators" and a drop down list will appear

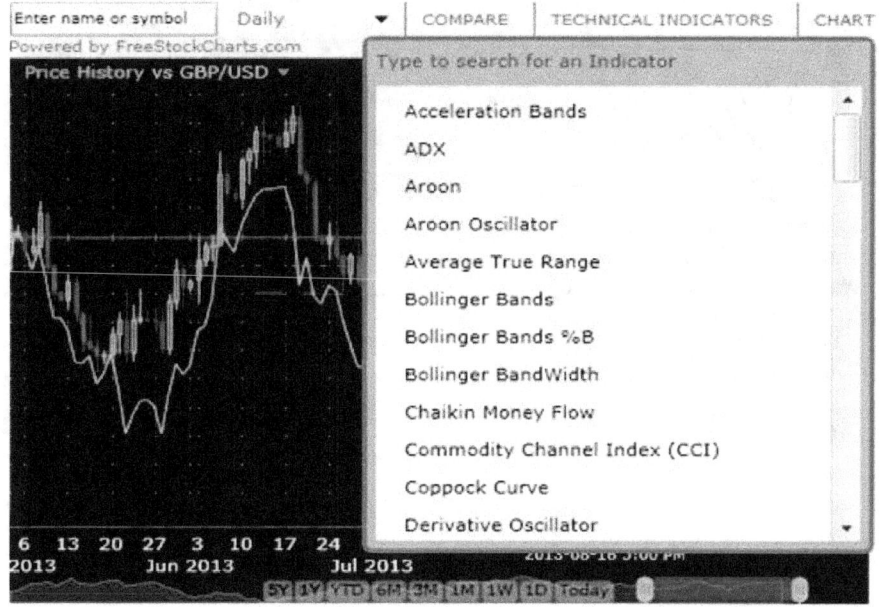

Pick your indicator, and it will be applied to your chart. Each indicator is customizable and in many cases can be applied to the price history or another indicator. Usually, you'll want to add the indicator to the price history, so when you pick an indicator and it asks you where you want to apply it, choose "Price History".

All the indicators you have added will show along the bottom of the price chart, or on the price data. To customize the indicator, click on the little arrow next to indicator name and choose "Edit."

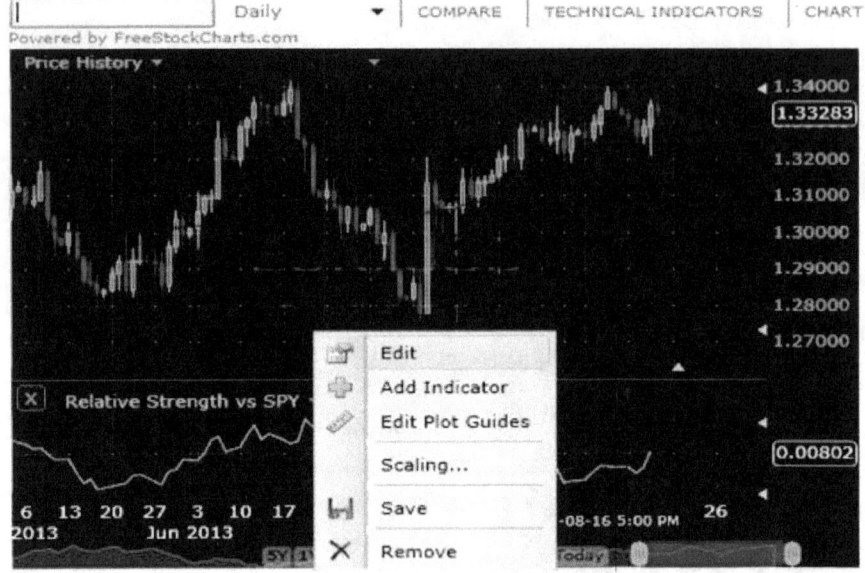

Zoom in and Out

One of the great features of Free Binary Options Charts is how easy it is to zoom in and out, seeing longer-term or short-term trends.

Quickly zoom in and out on the time frame you are watching by pulling the gray sliders at the very bottom of the chart to the right or left respectively. You can even go back in time and zoom in on a specific day in the past using these sliders.

You can also quickly change your overall time frame by clicking on one of the gray bottoms at the bottom, such as 1Y (1 year), YTD (year-to-date), 6M (6 months) or 1D (1 day)

Settings

Finally, you can customize the overall setting of free binary options charts by selecting "Chart" on the upper right. Most of these settings you don't need to worry about too much, except for the first setting which you may want to change based on personal preferences.

By default, the "Price Style" is set to Candlestick. Candlestick charts are the preferred type of chart for many traders. If you prefer a different type of chart you can also select Line, OHLC (OpenHighLowClose) Bar, HLC (HighLowClose) Bar, or Bar. All these types of charts show the price history, but in different visual ways and some contain more information than others. For example, candlestick charts show much more detail price information than a line chart.

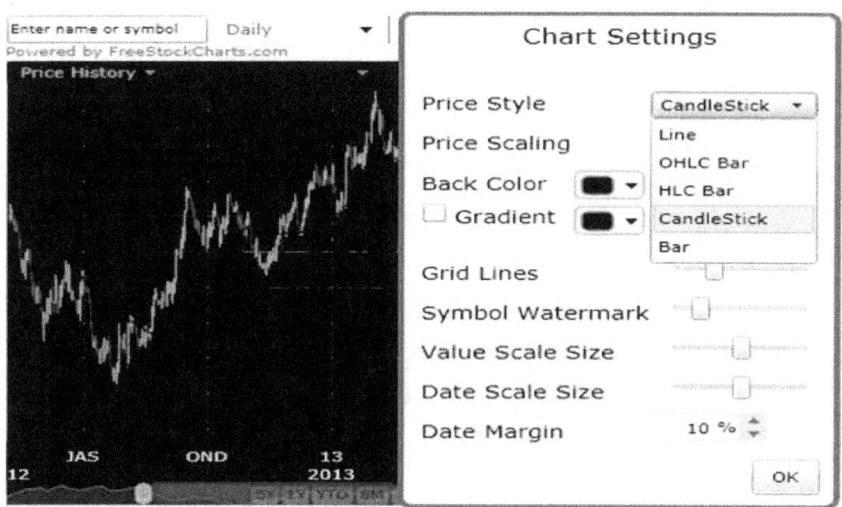

A combination of both

Despite the fundamental differences between the two major analysis methods, there are many traders who adopt a mixed trading style. Generally, these market players base their decision making on fundamental analysis but determine the best possible entry and exits points according to their technical analysis. They also take into account major technical support and resistance levels, including previous highs and lows, as well as moving averages (and moving average crossovers) and others, to predict where the price is likely to halt momentum and rebound, or possibly accelerate further if it penetrates through the respective price level.

Chapter 5: Binary Options Strategies And Techniques For Beginners

3 Binary Options Trading Strategies For Beginners

If you've studied and understood my previous posts about the fundamentals of binary option FX trading and binary options indicators, you are now ready to trade for real. Here are 3 different strategies that I use, choose one based on your risk appetite. Good luck!

Conservative Long-term Strategy

This strategy is for those who are new to this game and want to build up their capital slow and steady. The point of this strategy is to minimize risk and wait for the perfect setup on the chart.

In this case the perfect setup is using the ZigZag's last 2 points, and draw a Fibonacci between them in the direction of the trend.

Draw your fibo from point 1 to point 2 for a down trend, and vice versa for an uptrend. Your target is 161.8 projection level.

In order for the signal to be fully valid, there has to be a retracement to between 50 – 88.6. The higher the retracement goes, the stronger the signal. In the example above, the retracement happens next to the number 2 in the upper left corner.

The key here is to be patient until all 3 factors line up.

The entry rule is:

- Price hits Fibonacci projection level 161.8.
- Price is inside or outside of the bounds of the red channel.
- Value Chart hits level 8 or above

Your Expiry can be between 5 and 20 minutes. And your target is 1-2 trades per day.

And money management suggestion for this strategy is to take 2 equal bids per day for 20 days. Increase your position by 50% next day. If you lose, start with the last set of bids:

Day 1: 10 + 10

Day 2: 15 + 15

Day 3: 21 + 21... and so on. You should reach around 5k in profits within 20 days, and next month just start over or carry on from where you left.

Semi-Conservative Strategy

The semi-conservative strategy involves 4-6 trades per day. The rules are the same as for the conservative strategy, only with one exception: We take the trade at Fibonacci projection level 127 as well as 161.8.

Now, for level 127 trades, I would advise not to take the trade with more than 6 minutes to the expiry. This is because usually level 127 represents a consolidation level to draw buyers/sellers into the trend to get more liquidity and the price usually carries on in the direction of the trend within the next 3 candles.

The rules for entry are the same as with the conservative strategy:

—   Value Chart hits level 8

—   Price is inside the red zone

—   Price hits the Fibonacci 127 projection level

Use the same money management as with conservative strategy, but your earnings will increase faster.

And remember, You have to stick with the entry rules.

Now, the below strategy is a very aggressive one that defines the means of sane trading. This strategy represents the use of price cycles and Fibonacci sequence in fast trading. Trades are not only taken at levels 127 and 161.8 but also at breakouts. And Fibonacci levels are drawn for every cycle. This strategy also exploits the full potential of value charts.

Above you learned what you are hunting, where to find your prey, and how to bag some prey steady and safe. Now, we will go after the BIG 5.

Aggressive Strategy

Look at the chart below, how many price cycles do you see?

Yes, 9 cycles. Now, change your zigzag indicator parameters to 2,1,1. How many short-term price cycles do you see now?

Yup, 41+ short-term price cycles. In reality, there are much more, but let's not make it too difficult. Each of these cycles is a Fibonacci sequence with a high-low-retracement-projection-reverse. Look at the chart below:

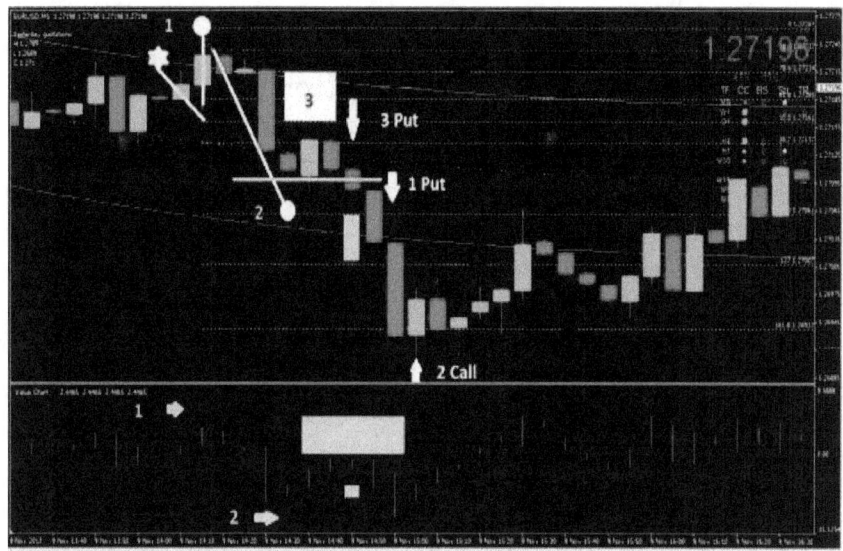

Now it gets complicated and wonderful:

The Fibonacci is drawn between points 1 and 2 (in light blue) and marked on value charts the last high and low, 1 and 2 respectively. Now we have the levels and waiting for the retracement which can be a wick or a full candle. Above the retracement area is the white box marked by 3, and the green candle underneath touches that box.

The setup is ready when the retracement candle is followed by a red candle in the direction of the trend. Now wake up.

The next red candle closes below the open of the green retracement candle, BUT it doesn't touch value chart level 6 yet, nor the regression channels inner band. This is marked by the light blue rectangle. So this is our first breakout candle of this specific sequence. We enter PUT 10 seconds before the close of this candle, as the next candle WILL BE BEARISH, with 90% probability. This is marked by 3 PUT on the chart above.

The next candle closes below our 100 Fibonacci level but DOES NOT TOUCH LEVEL 127, which means it closed below the low of our current sequence. We enter PUT 10 seconds before the close of this candle because it will be followed by a bearish candle or 2-3 bearish candles which will reach level Fibonacci level 161.8. This trade is represented on the chart by 1 PUT.

The last bearish candle hits Fibonacci level 161.8 and value chart level -8 and also the outline of the red zone, so we place a CALL.

Within each price cycle between 3 points there are on average 3 ITM trade setups during normal volatility trading conditions. And for this strategy, it goes without saying that if you don't 'feel' the trade or something about the setup doesn't seem right, don't take it and wait for the next one.

This strategy will produce around 100 setups per currency pair per day, so use it wisely, and be very sure to learn it by heart before you jump in full steam.

The 3 strategies explained here work for all currency pairs, commodities, stocks and indices. However, even with the conservative strategy, a trader can produce excellent results if they trade 5-6 assets, and take 2 high probability trades per asset per day.

Other Strategies

You can choose to trade in a variety of different option types or stick to one. It is advisable, especially when you are new to trading, to stick to just one at a time. This will help you to develop your understanding of the specific asset and improve your trading ability. There are several strategies which can help you make the most of every potential trade:

Trend strategy

This strategy is a tried and tested way of investing in the market regardless of whether the price of your chosen asset is moving up or down. The key to employing this tactic effectively is preparation, you will need to study the market and, preferably, plot the rise and fall off either a market sector or a specific asset. The more data you can collect the more accurate your chart will be; the chart will show the rise and fall of the item and you should be able to see a pattern forming. The general pattern is likely to go in one direction; up or down. If you go far enough back with your data you may notice that the price rises for several days or weeks and then drops for a similar period. If you can locate a pattern of ups and downs you have found the trend and can use this to buy and sell your trade at the right time.

This trend will show you when you can buy and predict an increase in price and when you should expect it to decrease. It is possible to make a good profit when prices are moving in either direction.

Pinocchio strategy

This strategy is used if you think the price of a chosen asset is about to go up or down by a large amount. You will need to study market data to decide the right time to purchase, you will be going against the current trend; timing will be very important. This is a good strategy to practice without risking money, either by monitoring the stock prices or by using a demo account.

Straddle Strategy

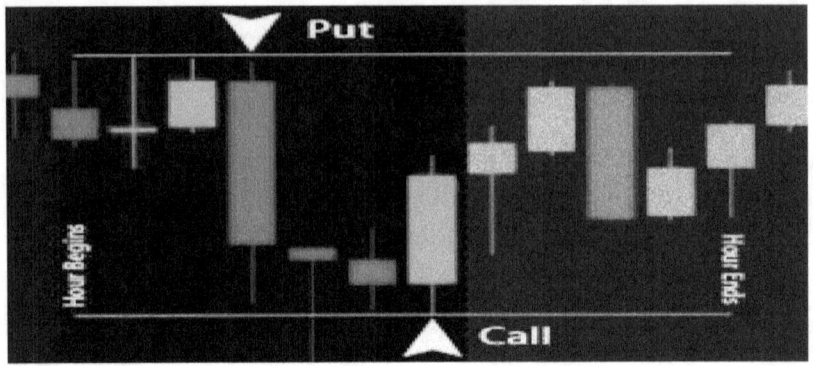

This is the technique to use when the market is experiencing a lot of movement up and down or everyone is waiting for a specific piece of news.

This can be a difficult strategy to get right but it can be very effective. Uncertainty, the market will often prompt rapid changes in the direction of the price. The trick is to locate an asset which you believe is about to go down in value, but which is currently increasing. At the opportune moment, you need to purchase an option that the price will decrease; as soon as it starts to decrease you buy a second option which assumes it will rise. In effect you are straddling the market, your options should be bought on or very close to the peaks and troughs and expire near the opposing rise or fall. It is advisable to practice this without risking your capital.

Risk Reversal Strategy

This involves buying an option for the price to increase and one for it to decrease at exactly the same time. This approach is usually adopted when the asset price is showing a lot of movement. You are effectively trading that it will both rise and fall; one of your trades will be correct!

Hedging Strategy

Binary Hedging/Straddle Strategy

Applying the hedging/straddle binary options strategy is comprised of a simultaneous trade on one asset in opposite directions. This trading strategy includes risk management features which prevent you from enduring a full loss of your traded invested capital and the substantial chance to profit. The strategy is based on the presumption that "what goes up, must come down", and it works as follows:

- Choose your general direction: decide if you wish to invest in a "Call" or a "Put" option.
- Choose your underlying asset and invest according to the general direction you earlier decided upon.

The trading strategy's tipping point; once the price of our underlying financial asset advances according to our predicted assumption, you make an opposing investment.

Despite the positive direction the trade has taken, traders ought to know that the potential threat of a sudden shift of the asset's general direction continuously lurks their trades. The accepted solution here would be to make an opposing investment.

If in step 1, your general direction leads you to invest in a "Call" option, in step 3 you will invest in a "Put" option. Consequently, you're now trading both "Call" and "Put" options, thereby minimizing the risk of losing on both options, and maximizing the chances of gaining from one of them.

In other words, the hedging binary trading strategy guarantees you'll end up "in the money"- its risk management in its finest form. To make things even better, if by the end of the trade the asset's market price was between the striking price of your first and second investments, you can actually end up benefiting from both trades.

Example:

The table below represents the USD/JPY price for a potential "Call" option. Let's assume the price will breach the descending trend line.

The price breaks the trend line and is retesting it before continuing its movement upward. Corresponding to the hedging strategy, at the retesting point, you invest in a "Call" option.

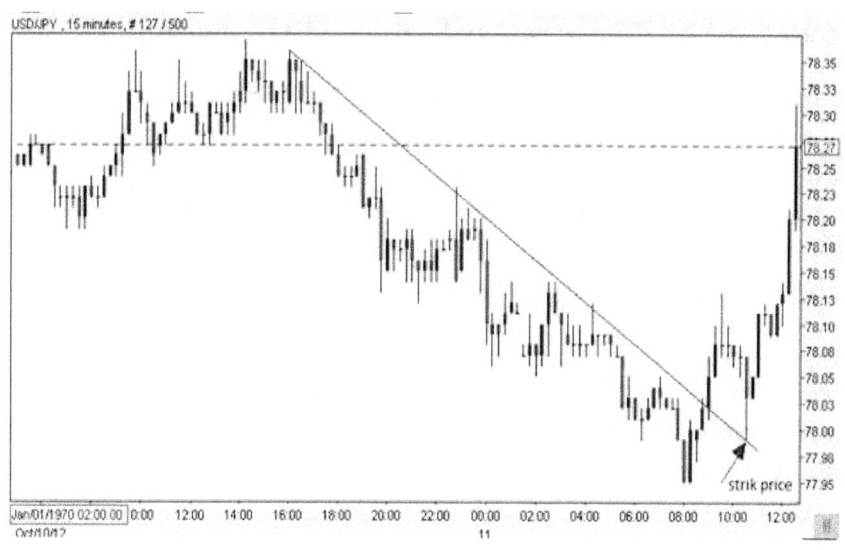

Once the price movement is corresponding to your prediction, i.e., the option is "In the Money", you wait for an opposing trend line to break again toward a decline. As a result, you lowered your risk and doubled your potential to profit

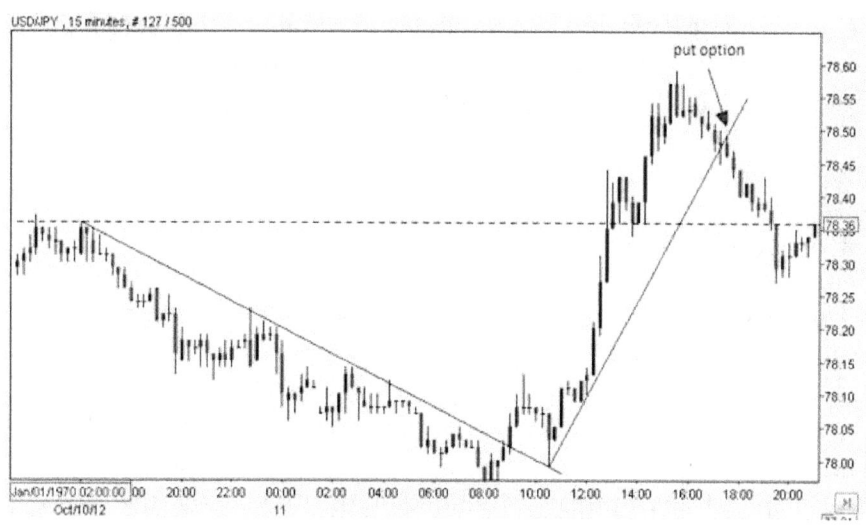

Hedging/Straddle Strategy Scenario Explanation

Normally, if you invest $200 in the USD/JPY option, as displayed on the chart above, and the asset's return is 85%, you either lose your $200, or alternatively, if you implement the above-mentioned strategy, in the event that the trade ends up "In the Money", you gain $170-even if one of the options expire "Out of the Money".

Applying the straddle binary strategy will spring different results to your trade. If all of the conditions are correct; the price movement is in your predicted direction and you're "In the Money"; you can take this investment to a whole new level by investing in an opposing "Call" option.

Generally speaking, there are 2 possible outcomes to this specific scenario:

- If the market's price either rises or falls over the striking price of the "Put" or "Call" options at the end of the trade's time frame, the trade ends "In the Money" for one option and "Out of the Money" for the other option. Hence, you made $170 and lost $200, leaving you with a loss of $30.
- In the event that the market's price stays between the striking price of the "Call" and "Put" options, the outcome would be a gain of $340.

Correction Binary Strategy

During the beginning and ending of round hours, assets tend to undergo unexpected surges (both upwards and downwards). These surges also occur prior to, during, and after important market announcements and are exactly what you should look for in order to apply the Correction binary trading strategy. The principle of this strategy is founded on the Correction rule. The rule states that if a price of an asset surges upwards or downwards and a gap appears between the current and previous price of the asset, the asset will then correct itself, and return back (close the gap) to its previous price.

Now that you know how the Correction rule affects an asset's market price, it is possible to leverage from it. Using the graphs' support and resistance lines, or the trend line that appears in technical analysis, you can identify price gaps. The Correction strategy asks you to detect such gaps and then execute a binary option trade in the opposite direction.

This strategy works on a similar basis to risk reversal, buying an option for the price to go up and simultaneously buying one for the same asset to go down in value. This will ensure that one of your trades has a positive outcome and will minimize any losses.

Chapter 6: Beginner Binary Options Winning Strategy

It's a little bit awkward to talk about a particular and well-established binary options winning strategy given the fact that this strategy doesn't really have any name at all. However, let's call it beginner binary options winning strategy because effectively this is what it is. Read below to find out how this could be the best binary options strategy for beginners and what you will have to do in order to use it.

This strategy works by predicting the future movement of an asset taking in consideration the data supplied by four financial trading indicators. These indicators are mentioned below.

The indicators listed below are automatically generated by the charting feature offered by most binary options brokers. It is extremely important to only register at binary options brokers that have these indicators (like the ones we listed in the top list table above) otherwise you will not be able to use this strategy.

It's also not really necessary to fully understand what these indicators precisely are in order to be able to use this strategy. If you want a full description of these indicators please check out our related article.

You can find the indicators listed below:

- 13 Exponential Moving Average (EMA)
- 20 Simple Moving Average (SMA)
- 26 Exponential Moving Average (EMA)

These three indicators are represented by three lines that are moving around the line on the charting platform that represents the value of the asset itself.

Bollinger Band

The Bollinger Band, however, is represented by two lines. The middle of these two lines is the average of the position of the above-mentioned three indicators. So, basically, the Bollinger Band has two boundaries, an upper boundary and a lower boundary in which the above-mentioned three indicators are positioned.

How to use:

Now, let's talk about the actual strategy itself. As explained, with this strategy you will be able to predict the future movement of an asset.

In order to use this strategy, you will have to activate the above-mentioned indicators on your charting interface.

First, you will have to watch out for the following things:

- The 13 Exponential Moving Average (EMA) crosses the 20 Simple Moving Average (SMA)
- The 26 Exponential Moving Average (EMA) will cross the 20 Simple Moving Average (SMA) after which it will cross the 13 Exponential Moving Average (EMA)
- If the above conditions are met, then most of the time the following will happen:
- The value of the asset will go outside of one of the Bollinger Band boundaries.
- You will be able to tell which boundary the asset will cross based on the direction of the general movement of the above-mentioned three indicators.

If in average the three indicators (except the Bollinger Band) move up, then the asset will break the BB's upper boundary. If in average the three indicators will move down, then the asset will break the BB's lower boundary.

Like mentioned, the above-outlined scenario will happen around 80%-90% of the time, which is a lot but it also means that there will be cases when this prediction will be incorrect, so you should not assume that this strategy is a "sure win" – "sure win" strategies do not exist and anyone selling you one is lying.

Applicability of this Strategy

So, now you would want to know what exactly you would have to do in order to use this strategy to your advantage. There are actually multiple positions you could open in such cases. Let's take the example below.

- The exchange rate of EUR/USD is at 1.35 at this moment.
- The upper boundary of the Bollinger Band is at 1.37
- The lower boundary of the Bollinger Band is at 1.33

Now, you notice that the 13 EMA has crossed the 20 SMA and that the 26 EMA crossed the 20 SMA and is about to cross the 13 EMA soon.

You also notice that the three of these indicators are moving downwards.

In this case, you will know that during the next 15-30 minutes the value of EUR/USD will bounce BELOW the lower BB line; in other words, it will be below 1.33.

You will have to remember that after a short while the value of the underlying asset will always return back into the two boundaries of the Bollinger Band. There are basically two choices you can make in this situation.

    a) Buy a boundary option or a one-touch option and invest on the fact that the value of EUR/USD will hit a low boundary of at least 1.33. Remember, using this newbie strategy in most cases you will be able to predict that the asset will go below 1.33 the next 15-30 minutes.

This choice is a bit risky because you cannot know exactly when that event will happen during the next 15-30 minutes. However, purchasing a boundary option or a one-touch option can offer you extremely high payout rates of up to 500%. If you want to go safe, then buy a regular high/low option. if you are a beginner, then stick to high/low options for now.

    b) Buy a simple high/low option and bet on the outcome that in 15-30 minutes the value of the asset (in this case the exchange rate of EUR/USD) will be BELOW the current line (in this case 1.35).

This choice is less risky because the value of the asset will most likely go down during this time frame. By choosing a high/low option it is not relevant if the value of the asset will reach a specific value (in this case 1.33); it only matters that its value will decrease – and as the data from the strategy told us, the value will indeed most likely decrease in the majority of the cases.

If all this seems too complicated at first, you can try out a service such as Binary Options Robot initially. This will check the charts for you automatically for this and similar positions. You can then execute trades and learn to use this strategy yourself

Best applicability

So, at first read, the strategy might sound a little bit complicated to total newcomers who have never traded binary options or other instruments online. However, once you try it out yourself, it's actually not that complicated.

You will only have to watch the movement of the three indicators (13 EMA, 20 SMA, 26 EMA). You will have to enable these indicators on your charting interface in order to use them.

You will be able to tell which is which based on the color of the line representing them. You will only have to remember which color is which after which with a little practice you will be able to recognize them with ease.

Here is a color reference for these indicators:

- 13 EMA – Blue
- 20 SMA – Red
- 26 EMA – Cyan, light blue

The colors are usually the same at all brokers.

So, after watching these indicators, and you see the pattern mentioned above (13 WMA crossing the 20 SMA, 26 EMA crossing the 20 SMA after which crossing the 13 EMA) you will most of the time be able to predict the movement of the underlying asset (but remember, not always – nothing is guaranteed in financial trading).

If these three indicators collectively move up, then the asset will break the upper boundary of the BB (Bollinger Band). If these indicators show a downward trend movement, then the value of the asset will break the lower limit of the BB.

And it's really this simple. Use this, and you may be able to achieve a winning percentage that allows you to make profits. We believe that this is probably the best binary options strategy for beginners that is at this moment out there.

New: Long-term Binary Options Strategy for Beginners

As written in the final paragraph of the intro, I decided to also talk about a different beginner binary strategy. This strategy specifically focuses on binary options with long expiration times.

Essentially, this strategy works by you having to follow major news events related to the stocks of important companies and then make accurate long-term predictions.

Below you will find one example of how this strategy works:

You know that Apple will launch a new iPhone on October 1st. You also know that usually, this will result in an increase in Apple's stock prices the next day.

Around two weeks before this event takes place, you buy a binary options contract that predicts that Apple's stocks will increase by October 2. And boom, you just won because this prediction will very likely come true.

You can do this strategy with hundreds of other companies and with other assets as well other than stocks. You need to check which major news events are upcoming during the next few weeks and months and make long-term predictions.

I actually believe that this strategy is even easier than the initial Bollinger band strategy described above. With this strategy you don't have to use charts and indicators; you'll only have to wait for major news events to happen (expected product launches by companies, annual revenue reports, etc.).

You can find a full description of this strategy by reading this article.

Learn More About Binary Options Strategies

These are just two of the many binary options winning strategies for beginners available. I felt that these ones were the simplest strategies available, so if you are new to binary options then you should begin with mastering these strategies.

Conclusion

This book will equip you with all the necessary basics tools, strategies and techniques required to dominate binary trading options as a beginner. As you read about additional and more advanced strategies, your chances of increasing your winning margin are totally guaranteed.

Remember, binary options trading is not about luck, it's about strategy and knowledge. Wishing you the best in your trading.

www.ingramcontent.com/pod-product-compliance
Lightning Source LLC
Chambersburg PA
CBHW060414190526
45169CB00002B/892